THE GIVING GARDEN

How nonprofit organizations can maximize donor giving
through customized cultivation pathways

By Sandi Frost Steensma
with Julie Hordyk

Kennari Consulting
Grand Rapids, MI

© 2022 Sandi Frost Steensma

All rights reserved. No part of this publication may be reproduced, stored in a retrieval system, or transmitted in any form or by any means electronic, mechanical, photocopying, recording or otherwise, without the prior written permission of the publisher.

Published by
Kennari Consulting | Grand Rapids, MI

Publisher's Cataloging-in-Publication Data
Steensma, Sandi Frost.

The giving garden : how nonprofit organizations can maximize donor giving through customized cultivation pathways / Sandi Frost Steensma with Julie Hordyk. – Grand Rapids, MI : Kennari Consulting, 2022.

p. ; cm.

ISBN13: 978-0-9601123-0-2

1. Fund raising--Management. 2. Nonprofit organizations--Management. 3. Benefactors. I. Title. II. Hordyk, Julie.

HV41.2.S74 2022
658.15224--dc23

Project coordination by Jenkins Group, Inc. | www.jenkinsgroupinc.com

Cover design by Kathy Bustard. Illustration by Susan M. Rose.

Printed in the United States of America
25 24 23 22 21 • 5 4 3 2 1

Contents

Acknowledgments ....
Introduction 1
One: What Makes a Gorgeous Garden? 3
Two: Find the Focal Points 10
Three: Start with Seedlings 18
Four: Stock the Wheelbarrow 26
Five: Build a Hive 36
Six: Start Pollinating! 45
Seven: Keep the Bees Happy! 53
Eight: Find Joy in the Work 61
Nine: Reflections of a Gardener 72

Acknowledgments

Fundraising doesn't happen in a vacuum. It takes a village to create successful donor-centric strategies. In more than thirty years of fundraising, I've been fortunate to develop relationships with donors, volunteers, organizational staff, outside contractors, and consultant team members, weaving together networks for the benefit of many organizations. I am grateful for the opportunity to do this work with so many compassionate and thoughtful people.

This book is dedicated to all of you.

I am also grateful for our garden. Spending time in our garden made me think about donors as individual flowers that must be cultivated according to their specific and unique needs. Much of the writing of this book happened in a room overlooking the garden, where I watched plants grow and thrive from April through October. The natural beauty and drama helped me stop and think about these concepts.

This book is dedicated to gardeners everywhere, whose loving work showcases the principal of individual cultivation in breathtakingly beautiful ways. Special thanks to Jack Barnwell, who designed the stunning garden that surrounds our home on Mackinac Island. It was the inspiration for this book.

Sandi Frost Steensma

INTRODUCTION

I have spent virtually my entire professional career in fundraising. And I love it. When I'm in a meeting, I'm often the only one in the room who can say that! I am passionate about helping nonprofit organizations, and the professionals who work in them, find joy and success in the work.

This book arises both from my passion and my experience in philanthropy. I decided it was time to share my "giving garden" concept after being inspired by the garden in front of my home. I hope that, through this book, I can help more people and organizations achieve fundraising success.

My purpose is simple. I want to help organizations transition to donor development strategies that have the highest return on investment and create the most committed, loyal donor base. I have used this methodology for many years and have adapted it to work with any organization. I've applied these strategies to small nonprofits with an annual budget of $60,000, and to multi-million dollar fundraising giants. These strategies, tools, and tactics work for any organization in any geographic market. Even relatively successful organizations raise more money when they follow these guiding principles.

Most of these concepts were developed after the recession of 2008. That event changed fundraising forever in some very profound ways. Donors were concerned about essential needs first and foremost, but they were also concerned about organizations they loved and supported in areas like education, arts and culture, and healthcare. They focused on organizations making the most impact, and they became less interested in attending fundraising events that weren't related to an organization's mission. This shift drove a corresponding fundraising transition from transactional models to relationship-based models. Donors wanted to learn more about how organizations achieved their missions. They wanted to roll up their sleeves and become engaged. Events, while they still have a place in our work, became less important. Building relationships became more important. We had to fundamentally change how we do our work

These principles held true and were put to the test once again during the writing of this book, as we all dealt with the coronavirus pandemic. The clients who were using this approach adapted very quickly to the demands of crisis fundraising. They were more flexible, more resilient, and better able to communicate individually with their most important donors.

The concepts might feel uncomfortable because they are counterintuitive to other philanthropic approaches. And it may seem, initially, like this approach would take longer. However, I have found that the strategies outlined in this book elicit the best return on investment in all kinds of fundraising: annual giving, campaigns, and endowment building. Ultimately, the fundraising goes faster because the gifts are larger. So although the pace may seem slow at first, your organization will see rapidly increasing results as it moves forward!

Each chapter teaches a concept, including real-life examples from my personal experience. And since my goal is to cultivate better "donor gardeners," I end each chapter with something "From the Toolshed" that can be used to analyze and impact your organization's work.

Let's start gardening!

Sandi Frost Steensma
Founder
Kennari Consulting

ONE: WHAT MAKES A GORGEOUS GARDEN?

> *"A garden requires patient labor and attention. Plants do not grow merely to satisfy ambitions or to fulfill good intentions. They thrive because someone expended effort on them."*
>
> — Liberty Hyde Bailey, Co-Founder, American Society for Horticultural Science

To the uninitiated, a lush flower garden full of eye-popping color and stunning plants may seem like a happy accident. We might say, "Wow, that gardener sure has a green thumb!" And while that's probably true, we're demonstrating that we don't understand how such a beautiful garden came to be.

Gorgeous gardens don't happen by accident. A skilled gardener employs a variety of strategies to achieve results. He or she carefully chooses plants of differing heights and complementary colors, and places them perfectly and precisely for maximum effect. Then each plant receives individual watering, fertilization, and pruning based on its own needs. All of this planning and care yields, over time, the jaw-dropping beauty that only a masterfully managed garden can deliver. It takes more than luck to create a garden that will turn heads. It takes patience, planning, focus, and individual care. The same is true in fundraising.

Every organization has its own unique garden of donors. Here, in our first chapter, it's important to begin thinking of donors as individuals, not as a group. We always hear things like, "Let's send them all a letter," or "Let's invite them all to an event, " as though each person has exactly the same interests and needs. To really understand these concepts, it's important to see donors not as a group, but as individual types of flowers in your organization's philanthropic garden.

Donors are like individual flowers that need specialized attention, or cultivation. But it's easier to treat all donors the same way. Many of us learned the pre-2008 practices, when transactional fundraising was the rule rather than the exception. Soliciting donors with appeals, sending newsletters, and mounting fundraising events have been the cornerstones of fundraising for decades. Why? It takes less time and seems more efficient. And time, as we all know, is the bane of the fundraiser's existence. There's never enough time!

How does a "one size fits all" strategy impact donor giving? Let's go back to our garden analogy.

Imagine a gardener who is stretched for time and has too many other priorities. He or she might set sprinklers to water the whole garden for thirty minutes every day. Next, in the interest of time, all the plants might get a dose of the same fertilizer three times per year.

What's going to happen to this carefully curated collection of plants? Most will droop and eventually die. Those that need very little moisture will drown in the daily watering. Those that slurp up great amounts of water will die of thirst. Plants that thrive on more regular feedings will be small and unhealthy. Those that need very little in the way of additional minerals will overdose and choke. A few will thrive. By sheer luck, the chosen combination of water and fertilizer will be perfect for some plants.

Ultimately, the garden will lose the wondrous variety that made it so stunning in the first place. Instead of a garden, you'll have a patch of daisies (or whatever thrives in those conditions).

The same is true for the fundraising garden. Generally speaking, the "one size fits all" approach of traditional philanthropy can produce rather frustrating and anemic results. Donor relationships don't grow. Gifts are smaller than they could be. So even though the organization spends a lot of time and money on these activities, it is not getting the return it hoped for, or the resources it needs to fulfill the mission. The donor garden isn't thriving.

So here's what I have learned. Donors, like flowers, all need different kinds of care to thrive. A *customized cultivation pathway* for each donor yields those eye-popping philanthropy results that every fundraising professional and every nonprofit organization wants to achieve.

~ An Illustration ~

My long-term work with an arts organization provides a good example of how customized cultivation pathways can lead to incredible results.

This organization was ready to mail information about an endowment campaign to feasibility study participants in September of 2008. And then the market crashed, leading to an extended recession. Conventional wisdom would have been to "wait it out."

We did put a pause on the campaign itself. Instead, we utilized this unique gift of time and went to work on donor cultivation to ensure that the eventual campaign would be even more successful. We formulated a list of their prospects using past giving history and community giving history as our guide. We created a Donor Development Committee. (Note that I didn't call it a Fundraising Committee — more on that later.) This committee worked through that list week after week, gathering information about each person and why they supported this organization. Through that process, we came to understand that donors gave to the organization for widely differing reasons. Some people believed the organization was good for the community. Others believed the organization enhanced education. Still others liked that the organization attracted people with similar interests. Still others just loved the art form.

The committee was able to formulate specific cultivation opportunities for the top 50 prospects list that addressed these different motivations and reasons for giving. For example, they took people behind the scenes to meet the director. They engaged hosts who then invited selected people to intimate small ensemble performances in their homes. Since many of the donors and donor prospects travel to Florida in the winter, they engaged performers to plan programs that could be taken on the road. Still other prospects were invited to watch rehearsals. The organization spent almost *three years* designing and implementing this cultivation plan. And a remarkable thing happened. During the worst economic downturn since the Great Depression, individual giving to this organization went up, and not just by a little. It went up *a lot*.

When the market started to recover, the organization initiated its campaign, now with many fully cultivated donors. Many people on the top 50 list gave significant gifts. Many of them also joined the campaign cabinet and played a key role in the campaign itself. And the organization raised the multi-million dollar target for their endowment campaign.

More than that, they have continued to use this method of donor cultivation for their annual giving. In the 12 years since creating their Donor Development Committee, they have more than doubled their annual fundraising from major donors.

The Lesson: In every single case, a customized cultivation pathway tailored to the donor's specific interests yielded significantly larger ongoing gifts. That's because the donors were fully engaged and invested in the organization's mission.

∼

Important Math

Here are a couple of things to remember. The first is that donors give, on average, to about a dozen organizations every year. However, the top three — those to which they are most deeply connected — receive about 80% of their total philanthropy. Our job in fundraising is to get into the top three! A customized cultivation pathway will greatly increase your organization's odds of winning one of those top spots.

Second, it's important to remember my favorite equation:

$$Resources + Inclination = The\ Gift$$

All of fundraising ultimately boils down to this simple equation. If there are resources and no inclination, there is no gift. Pretty simple. On the other hand, if there are few resources and great inclination, chances are your organization can land one of those coveted top three spots. Of course, the largest gifts will come from those with resources who are also highly inclined (or cultivated) to the organization.

Inclination is essential to the gift. I wish I had a dollar for every time someone has suggested we approach the Gates Foundation or MacKenzie Scott. After all, they are both giving away millions, even billions, of dollars. While they are giving away stunning amounts of money, they are giving it to organizations they know and trust; organizations with whom they have built strong relationships over many years. And if they don't know the organization itself, they are giving to organizations referred to them by people they know and trust. They're not giving money to just anyone!

Every nonprofit organization wants to include locally wealthy people on its donor list. There's a lot of competition for those dollars. But moderately well resourced people who care deeply about your organization can also give a lot of money. Don't overlook them! Your organization will do far better with people who have moderate resources and big inclination than it will with people who have huge resources but no inclination toward your organization's mission.

So how does your organization move donors to larger gifts? Work on the inclination side of the equation to increase annual (and campaign) gifts. In this book, I'm suggesting that customized cultivation pathways are the way to do just that.

Let's go back to the arts organization for a moment. They had a donor (we'll call her Lisa) who had been giving $1,000 annually. This is the threshold for a "major gift" in many organizations. The development director felt sure there was more potential. She knew Lisa had performed in high school, so she arranged for Lisa to sit with a professional and watch a rehearsal.

How did Lisa respond? "It was so amazing to sit next to a professional and see what it's like to follow a director. I was, honestly, kind of giddy with excitement! That kind of experience made me want to do everything I could to ensure the organization could reach more people. I can't believe I got to do that!" Ultimately, through this and other steps in the cultivation pathway, Lisa committed a much larger gift each year, and eventually made a planned gift to the organization.

Lisa reached this pinnacle of enthusiasm through a carefully crafted, customized cultivation pathway, not from one experience, and certainly not from a mass-mailed newsletter! And here's the best part: She was thankful for her experiences and *wanted to give*. Her emotional and personal connection to the organization skyrocketed, and her inclination soared.

This story illustrates the incredible power of the cultivation pathway approach. If your organization wants to achieve big results — and it wants a garden that's lush and colorful and vibrant — then it's time to start thinking about donors as individuals. Plan the work of individual cultivation and then work the plan.

I'm going to show you how.

From the Toolshed

Everyone in philanthropy likes metrics. One good way to measure your organization's effectiveness is to look at the average annual gift amount over time.

In the for-profit world, salespeople are driven by a goal. They know there are two ways to reach a sales target.

They can gain customers to increase their total sales, and/or they can sell more to existing customers.

Nonprofit organizations also have a revenue goal. It just has a different name. We call it our fundraising goal, or our annual giving goal. And we reach it in the same way a sales professional achieves his or her goal. We need to increase the net number of donors who give, and we need to increase the amount of the annual gift from our existing donors.

Here's a simple equation to help you think about fundraising effectiveness.

Total Gifts / Number of Donors = Average Gift

What does your organization's trend line look like as you plot it out year by year?

The average gift will go up if inclination is going up. Inclination goes up as your organization builds relationships and tells its story better. If the trend line is going up, congratulations! Keep doing what you're doing. (The caveat here is the average gift might also go up if the donor base shrinks. Make sure to look at the number of net donors, too.)

If the trend line is flat or (worse) heading downward, then this is the right book! It's time to revisit your organization's gardening strategies.

Two: Find the Focal Points

"A gardener's best tool is the knowledge from previous seasons. And it can be recorded in a $2 notebook."

— Andy Tomolonis, Horticultural Writer for the Boston Herald

Most gardeners will tell you that success requires planning. That's why a good gardener lays out a plan before he or she starts to dig, putting into practice lessons learned from past seasons. Focal points are essential to that plan. These are "wow factor" plantings that, by virtue of their color, size, or rarity, immediately attract attention.

Focal points are important for several reasons. They help direct the eye, and they lend coherence to what could otherwise be a riot of color and confusion with no discernable pattern. Perhaps more important, however, is the role that focal points play for the gardener. Those few plants command a lot of attention. The gardener must prioritize the needs of those plants because they hold the whole plan together. If the focal points fail to thrive, then the vision for the garden falls apart.

A successful and thriving philanthropic garden should have focal points, too. We call them major donors. Major donors are those who provide annual gifts at a significant level, often $1,000 and more, or campaign gifts that help complete a typical gift pyramid. Just as focal point plants command a disproportionate amount of a gardener's time, the subset of major gift prospects and donors should receive a significant portion of your organization's attention. The more time and attention they receive, the greater the return on investment will be. It's pretty simple, really.

However, many organizations feel they don't have the time or the tools to identify the focal points in their donor garden, much less spend time cultivating them. They have a large number of mostly undifferentiated donors who give relatively small gifts (in the $100-$1,000 range) in response to regular and ongoing transactional communications. They don't really have a garden per se. Everyone is treated the same.

So how do focal points get defined? A gardener selects the exact right plant, with the coloring, size, and blooming schedule that complements the overall garden plan and will thrive in a specific spot.

This work is a little harder for a nonprofit organization. Your organization needs to do two things in order to find its focal points.

First, create easy, mission-based ways to become a donor. Simple donor acquisition activities are the way for someone to start giving to your organization. Each organization should have a few ways for donors to engage with first-time gifts. Those methods should reach people in different ways, but always remain focused on the mission.

Traditional transactional events can be sources of donor acquisition. A gala is a good example, because it offers people the chance to make a gift during the event. However, these types of events don't usually reap the long-term results that mission-focused events do, unless there is specific follow-up for the newly acquired donor. Other traditional events, like a golf event or a run, will attract golfers and runners. While the proceeds of these events can help support the organization, they often don't attract first-time donors specifically interested in your organization's mission. (The exception, of course, is an organization like Girls on the Run or First Tee, for example. In those cases, a run or a golf outing might be the perfect donor acquisition activity because it is mission-related.) Regardless of what they are, transactional events can be quite time-consuming and often require a specific skill or talent. They can be an expensive way to acquire those first-time donors.

To be truly mission-focused and gain first-time donors who have mission inclination, donor acquisition activities should have three important features:
- They should be connected to the organization's mission.
- They should require no more than an hour or two of the attendee's time.
- They should be promoted as fundraising events and include a clear and direct ask.

We'll talk more specifically about mission-specific donor acquisition activities in Chapter Three.

The second thing that the organization needs to do is comb through its donor list to find highly inclined donors. I can almost guarantee there are people with substantial capacity hiding in your organization's donor database. You just need to find them!

~ An Illustration ~

When I think about an undifferentiated donor database, I think of a radio station we worked with in the past. Like similar organizations, their donor database was massive…thousands and thousands of names. That's because they held a successful broad-based donor acquisition event twice per year, during which they would invite listeners to support their mission. This event would yield hundreds and hundreds of gifts, many of them under $500. Each of the donors gave because they loved the radio station, so it was a perfect donor acquisition activity. Unfortunately, the folks at the station could not possibly know which of these donors had more capacity and potentially more inclination toward the station. They had that many donors.

We started by pulling the list of donors who had given $500 or more during the on-air drive. Our assignment was to learn more about them and why they loved the radio station. Why $500? It's a fairly sizeable gift for a broad-based appeal. A gift at that level showed a worthy amount of inclination as well as capacity.

Many of the donors were familiar to me, as well as to some of the organization's key volunteers, so we placed them on our top prospects list for further review. But one donor jumped out at me. I happened to know that this couple (let's call them the Smiths) had been involved in other organizations and might be interested in being similarly involved with the radio station.

With that knowledge in hand, we put together a customized cultivation pathway for the Smiths. We invited them to a concert of a performer they loved. Then they hosted a house party with that same musician. Next up was a national radio conference. Over a period of four years, the Smiths became substantial annual donors. They also poured their efforts into a very successful capital campaign to build a new home for the radio station.

It's important to understand that this kind of intentional, personalized cultivation leads to joy for the donor. The Smiths didn't have to be coerced to serve! They loved the radio station even more as they journeyed along their customized cultivation path. They *wanted* to give. They said, "We know this station will bring truth and encouragement to thousands of people each year."

The Lesson: Your organization may already have one or more potential major gift donors in the database. Time spent researching existing donors is a great place to start. Once your organization identifies those major donor prospects, it can begin to develop the customized cultivation path that will increase their inclination and, eventually, their gift.

Practical Tips for Choosing Your Focal Points

A gardener needs to research the options to find exactly the right focal points for the climate, soil, and conditions of the garden. Organizations need to do research on their major gift prospects as well.

I always recommend that clients start with their existing donor list. If the list is not too large, work with the whole thing. If, like the radio station, your organization has an extensive list, then use some filters to pare it back a bit. Typical filters could include size of past gifts, number of years of giving, or frequency of giving.

Next, find some people who can contribute bits of intelligence about the donors on that list. I want to emphasize three important things I've learned about how to find the most promising major gift donor prospects.

1. **Don't assume.** Someone who lives frugally may have significantly more capacity than they appear to have. In fact, that simple lifestyle may provide more disposable income than is available to someone with a big mortgage and multiple car payments. In addition, someone who is already on your organization's major gift list might have substantially more potential than his or her past gifts indicate. And don't forget about the massive transfer of wealth that's happening as Baby Boomers leave their estates to the next generation. The "millionaire next door" is a real thing. We rarely know who just inherited significant wealth. Even something as massively disrupting as the coronavirus pandemic rarely provides clues as to individual wealth and capacity. Yes, many people were hurting, and many did not have the ability to give. But others were just fine. I had more than one donor tell me after those initial months of shock, "Honestly, we're doing okay." If we had assumed that everyone was in financial trouble, many gifts would have been missed and many organizations would not have survived.

2. **Keep the list manageable**. Customized cultivation pathways require time and effort to plan and execute. So set your organization up for success! If one or two people are tasked with the work, I recommend starting with 10-12 donors/prospects. If the organization has more capacity, choose more names. Just remember that each of these people will require individualized, regular attention. If the list feels overwhelming, it will be tempting to start treating everyone the same way. Quite frankly, that's exactly what we are trying to avoid. That's the recipe for daisies in the garden, not beautifully cultivated focal points.
3. **Be curious**. No one source of information is going to shine the spotlight on the organization's best prospects. The tiniest detail can reveal a universe of information that will shape the cultivation pathway. Check many sources. Ask a small team of people for intelligence about donors on the list. (Look for more information about those people in Chapter Five.)

From the Toolshed

I've already mentioned this, but it bears repeating: curiosity is your best friend. It takes a lot of research to gain a realistic picture of a donor's potential capacity and their interest in your organization's mission. For example, an orchestra would want to know if their potential donor played an instrument or loves orchestral music. A substance abuse treatment facility would find it meaningful to know if someone in the donor's family has struggled with addiction. Connection to the mission is the single biggest indicator that inclination can be built over time. And that just may be the most important point in this book.

Here are some of the information sources you might think about using to gain insight about donors.

- **Wealth audit**. These reports used to be the exclusive domain of universities and hospitals. Now they are cost-effective enough for most nonprofits to use. A wealth audit pulls information from the public domain. This includes stock holdings, real estate ownership, gifts to political campaigns, charitable gifts, and more. Use this data to give an indication of total wealth. How much income is needed to support this lifestyle? This report can help your organization decide who in the donor list might warrant additional research. Keep in mind that these types of reports are not completely accurate, due to how they are derived. However, they can help provide guidance on who to cultivate.

- **Giving history**. Look at the giving history of the people in your organization's donor database. If someone has given to you for a long time, or gives many times during the course of a year, they definitely have inclination. If it has been some time since the last gift, or if someone made a single gift, the donor may have given a memorial, honorary, or event gift rather than one stemming from personal interest in your organization's mission.
- **Internet searches**. I realize that not everything you read online is accurate. However, a simple web search may yield very interesting information about the donor prospect.
- **Local news archives**. Some newspapers offer a search function through their past editions. Others require you to have a subscription. The library often carries local newspaper archives, as well as other potential sources of information. Articles, obituaries, and other notices can provide information about a donor prospect and his or her philanthropic interests.

Try practicing this a bit on someone from your organization's current donor list. Pick a donor who you think might have some potential to make more or larger gifts. Run a wealth audit. Do some research. See what can be learned about that person, and compare it to what resides in the donor database. This exercise will make it very clear why identifying and cultivating these focal points is going to require time and energy. However, it will be well worth the effort!

Three: Start with Seedlings

> *"Don't judge each day by the harvest you reap,*
> *but by the seeds that you plant."*
> — Robert Louis Stevenson, Scottish Novelist and Poet

In the last chapter, I explained the importance of having a plan and focal points to create a gorgeous and diverse garden. I also promised that we would talk about finding those donors who will make up your organization's garden. After all, the plan is a critical first step, but there's more work to come. The garden doesn't grow itself.

The plants themselves transform a paper plan into a gorgeous garden. The last thing a gardener would do is prepare the soil and then sit back waiting for plants to magically appear. That approach yields a nice crop of weeds, but not much else.

There are basically two ways to get plants for a garden. The first option is to buy some seeds, plant them in the ground or in small pots, and coax them to germinate. This takes a lot of time and effort. The second option is to visit a greenhouse and snag some seedlings. This is a much faster way to get the garden going.

In fundraising, donors and donor prospects are the plants. Just as no gardener would wait for random plants to grow in a plot of dirt, an organization should not simply wait for donors to "appear." Deliberate and strategic cultivation is needed to bring people into the donor garden.

Coincidentally enough, there's a "seed" way and a "seedling" way to do this.

In my experience, direct mail can be similar to the seed approach. Many nonprofit organizations buy a mailing list and send out solicitation letters. The people on the mailing list have very little connection to the mission. It's no surprise, then, that the response rate to these kinds of mailings mimics a traditional marketing response. A typical unsolicited appeal mailing yields a .05% to 2% response, depending on how well the list is targeted. That result is not great, and it's frustrating for both the organization and the board. Yet organizations regularly go down this road. I get it. This route feels somehow less risky, more conventional. It feels safer.

However, I recommend a different starting point. Instead of beginning with random people, start by finding those who are already inclined to the mission. "How do I do that?" one might ask. "There's no such thing as a donor greenhouse."

Ah…but there is!

Think about it this way. The people already associated with your organization — its board, staff and volunteers — care deeply about the mission. They wouldn't give of their valuable time and talents if they didn't care. And they all have friends or acquaintances that might also be strongly inclined to care if they knew more. What's needed is a donor acquisition activity or event to get connected to those potential donors ("seedlings") whose interests and passions line up with your organization's mission and values.

An easy donor acquisition event is the best way to bring new donors into the garden. Let's look at an example.

~ An Illustration ~

In 2007, a local social work organization had just spun off from the county to become an independent nonprofit organization. Their entire donor database consisted of 50 donors in an Excel list. They had an initial operating budget of $60,000, with short-term support from the county. Clearly, they needed to find a lot more supporters to survive the transition.

We planned a donor acquisition event at the home of a prominent donor who supported the county's efforts to create the nonprofit entity. She provided the venue and the food. The organization formed a volunteer event committee, and those volunteers sent out 150 invitations to people they knew who might care about the mission. Approximately 70 people showed up to the first event. Those attendees nibbled wine and cheese, listened to a brief presentation about the organization's impact, and then were invited to support the mission through a gift. In one night, the organization more than doubled its donor database and raised $20,000!

That initial success was not a fluke. They repeated this event for five years, renewing donors and gaining new ones. Then they transitioned to a larger evening event that was still focused on their mission. Along the way, they've added other donor acquisition events as their capacity has grown. Today, they have more than 400 donors in their donor database.

The Lesson: The best way to gain new donors is to leverage the relationships of people who are already invested in the organization's mission. After all, people are most influenced by those they know and trust. A personal invitation to inclined prospects, combined with a mission-focused message, ultimately yields a high percentage of donors.

~

Guidelines for a Successful Donor Acquisition Event

I have helped nonprofit organizations plan hundreds of these events. The event can take different shapes, depending on the organization and its mission. I have seen people use lunches, house parties, progressive dinners, potlucks, mission-based movie premiers and more with great success. Here are the essential guidelines that each event should follow.

Use well-connected volunteers. Volunteers are the key to these events, because they each have a different web of personal connections. Make sure the volunteers are trained to invite guests who might be mission-oriented, not just their best friends. It's surprising how fast a list of donor prospects can grow if each volunteer identifies 5-10 people who might care about your organization's mission. Make sure the volunteers also do the inviting, since prospects are far more likely to say "yes" to a personal invitation from someone they know and trust.

Keep it short. The event should be no more than two hours, and one hour is even better. A small time commitment is a big attraction. We always hear after such events how much attendees appreciate that the organization valued their time.

Be honest. Tell folks right up front that this is a fundraiser.

Focus on the mission. Remember that a donor acquisition event should allow your organization to tell its story and make its case in a succinct yet compelling way. The more attendees understand the impact of your organization, the more willing they will be to make a gift. (Hint: personal testimonials from clients are one of the most powerful tools.)

Quantify services. Help attendees understand how gifts of different amounts impact one person. When prospects understand what they are supporting with their gift, they are inclined to give more. For example:

- $100 supports our program for one month
- $250 allows a child to attend our program for one year
- $500 provides services for 10 children
- $1,000 provides food for 10 families

Identifying each level with a unit of service helps donors understand how their gift can impact the people served by your organization. It also helps to communicate what constitutes a major gift for your organization. This gives those donors with more capacity a road map for making a greater impact with their gift.

Make a great ask. Don't skip this step! Have a non-staff person ask attendees to partner with your organization and support its mission. The more they feel the power of your work, the more inclined they will be to give. They will *want* to give!

Capture attendee information. Remember that the whole point of this exercise is to build the donor list with people inclined to the mission. Make sure there is a system for gathering name, address, phone number, and email address from each attendee.

Remember to ask for renewals. People who have heard your organization's story firsthand will remember that experience for a long time. I have found that first-time donor renewal rates are significantly higher after a mission-focused event than after any other event experience.

Sometimes creativity is required, especially when there are confidentiality issues related to the organization's work. The social work organization I referenced earlier is a great example. They were not able to bring the people they served to their luncheon due to confidentiality laws regarding their services. But they could have some of their volunteers change the names and share real stories. They could also have past clients talk about their experiences. Those stories hit home in a powerful way. They shared one story, in particular, about children who had been left in a closet most days. They were under-socialized to the point that they could not use utensils to eat. I overheard one attendee's quivering voice as she talked to her host. "I can't even imagine how it would feel to be 12 years old and never have been taught to use a knife and fork. Who would advocate for these kids if that volunteer wasn't there?" The stories she heard will stay with her for a long time.

Powerful stories, told in person, are a bit like a long-acting fertilizer for donors. They'll resonate long after the event is over and keep inclination blooming for your organization's cause.

Creativity also plays a role when there's an unexpected event like a pandemic. Spring is one of the busiest event seasons on the nonprofit calendar. The further we got into the coronavirus pandemic in the spring of 2020, the more obvious it became that in-person events were not going to happen. Many nonprofit organizations simply cancelled everything and tried to wait it out. We knew that was not the right solution. We had to help our clients approach events in a more creative way.

Some of our clients put together "Event in a Box" kits. One, whose fundraising theme revolved around a table, called these "Picnic Baskets." They included everything needed for a host to have small group events outdoors at his or her home once people felt more comfortable socializing. That basket included an electronic invitation, a "Menu" (agenda), the campaign brochure and video, and an "Ingredient List" (items that were needed for the project and could be funded). They even obtained gift cards for snacks from a local bakery.

Other clients created virtual versions of their traditional live events. It wasn't easy to boil an in-person event down to less than an hour of high-impact content, but many of our clients succeeded nicely. One library pulled together homemade iMovies featuring impact stories. They wrapped those into a scripted event with short presentations and a breakout room for small groups…all delivered via Zoom. They had over 100 attendees, many of whom were new to the organization. The attendance level clearly indicated that donor prospects were very interested. Imagine what the library would have missed if they had chosen to sit out this fundraising season! Now they have more people in their donor database who have a very memorable connection to the organization.

From the Toolshed

I'm pretty sure that every board I have ever worked with has initially balked at the idea of a donor acquisition event. It feels counterintuitive. They always say, "Let's just send a letter."

Okay. It's time to look at the rough math of acquiring 50 new donors through a mailing vs. an event. These numbers are not meant to be exact, but rather to illustrate a point. You can plug in specific costs to arrive at a more accurate estimate. Keep in mind:

- An excellent response rate to a purchased direct mail list (i.e., people who are not already on your mailing list) is 2%, and the average gift is about $48.
- In my experience, the number of people making a gift at a donor acquisition event is, at minimum, 60%, and the average gift is at least $150.

The ROI of a Mailing

Purchase a mailing list of 2,500 names	$125
Print and mail a letter (with envelope)	$3,000
Total Cost	$3,125
Estimated gifts (50 gifts of $48 each)	$2,400
Total profit (loss)	($725)

The ROI of a Donor Acquisition Event

Create a volunteer-identified list of 150 attendees	$0
Design electronic invitations that volunteers can email	$100
Venue and food	$3,000
Total Cost	$3,100
Underwriting	$3,000
Sponsorships	$4,000
Major gifts	$3,000
Estimated gifts (90 gifts of $150 each)	$13,500
Total Proceeds	$23,500
Total profit (loss)	$20,400

One doesn't have to be an accountant to understand this math! And though there is also staff time to consider, I've also seen much higher results from these events over the years. The amounts listed are just minimums to show a starting point and demonstrate results for the first year of an event. By adding a strong major gift component to the ask — with levels attached to units of service — and a few sponsorship levels on the front end of the event, organizations can do even better. We have seen clients exceed $100,000 in gifts with events of this type. That's a pretty nice impact for a one-hour event!

Event donors are also much more likely to renew the next year. That means it's good math now, and even better math over time. Do the math for a few of your organization's development efforts and consider what adjustments could be made.

Four: Stock the Wheelbarrow

"I mean, if we even had a wheelbarrow, that would be something."
— William Goldman, "The Princess Bride"

Picture an experienced gardener tending to the plants. He or she trundles along from place to place, stopping at the plants that need care. Some need feeding. Others are thirsty. A few might need to be divided or pruned. At each stop, the gardener rummages through the wheelbarrow and pulls out the perfect tools for the job at hand. That gardener can tend to many different plants' needs with a relatively small collection of basic tools. That might include gloves, pruning shears, a small shovel, plant food, and a watering can.

The wheelbarrow is an important concept for donor cultivation work. It holds a flexible collection of tools that can be used while tending the cultivation pathway for each donor. There are two important points to understand about the wheelbarrow.

This first one might feel a little counterintuitive (again) but it's true. While each donor cultivation pathway is unique, they are all built using a common set of tools. Stop and absorb that idea for a moment. It's not necessary to invent a new or unique *tool* for every donor. What's important is that each *pathway* is customized to the donor. Gardeners don't fill the wheelbarrow so that it's overflowing with every gadget ever invented. They use a relatively small number of tools to accomplish virtually all the essential work. The same is true for nonprofit organizations. It's better to invest time and some resources into a few good multipurpose tools. We'll get to that list of tools later in the chapter.

This leads to point two. The tools may be the same, but the way they're used is different for each donor. This is where the individual cultivation pathway comes into play. Let's think about the garden again. Our master gardener isn't going to use all the tools on each plant. For example, he or she might leave the daffodils alone after they're done blooming. Those bulbs need to draw nutrients from the spent leaves to fuel flowers next spring. However, each dead geranium will be cut immediately. This keeps the plant from wasting energy on a stem that has no more to give. In the same way, a nonprofit organization uses specific tools in the right sequence for each donor. They all should personally experience the life-changing work of your organization, but each of them will connect in a different way.

~ An Illustration ~

A hospital executive I know is super-accessible. He makes time in his calendar for intimate donor breakfasts and lunches. These give him a platform to share his deeply personal connection to the mission and his inspiring vision for the future. He sends what I term a "chatty letter" (not an ask) to selected donors a few times per year. He uses this method to keep in touch, sharing news about the organization's strategic direction and impact.

For many donors, knowing the leader of an organization matters a lot. They want to know the person, and where he or she is going. Leaders are not always the best ones to make an ask, but they are often powerful communicators who can inspire inclination in a donor.

Events such as small lunches or dinners are not complicated, especially when the CEO prioritizes them and is willing to invest time. Although they are simple, they are highly effective in the right situations. Here's a good example. After three years of individual donor and prospect cultivation work, this hospital received a one million dollar gift from a donor who initially attended breakfast with the CEO.

The Lesson: Access to a leader may cost time, but costs virtually nothing in dollars. However, it can be extremely effective with many types of people. It can inspire those who need to hear the message "right from the horse's mouth." It can breed confidence in someone who desires concrete information about strategic intent. And it can be a powerful platform for reaching donors who want the tough questions answered. The same tool addresses many different cultivation needs.

~

What Should Be in the Wheelbarrow?

"Starter kits" are popular, especially for do-it-yourself hobbyists. Search online for "gardening tools starter kit" and many of the essentials show up in one handy package. These are not the most sophisticated tools, but they are definitely the ones that a gardener will use over and over again. A starter kit makes it easy for beginners to address the most common needs.

I like to think of the following list as my "starter kit" for individual cultivation pathways. I've chosen these things for specific reasons:

Simplicity. These activities are not difficult to execute. Your organization might already have some of them, or perhaps can change what it already has in place to be more effective.

Impact. Cultivation is personal. These activities help connect the mission and values of your organization with the values of the donor. That builds inclination, which in turn increases giving.

Cost. These tools take some time to plan, but not a lot of money to put in place. In many cases, sponsors may underwrite the cost. Once they're developed, they can also be repeated without incurring extra cost.

Universality. Most organizations, regardless of size or mission, can figure out a way to creatively tell their story through these tools.

So what should be in your organization's wheelbarrow?

A tour. A concise, well-executed donor tour is one of the most powerful ways to connect donors to the mission. That's because tours provide concentrated time with the donor. A tour is a great opportunity to see and hear what triggers the most profound responses from donors. What's the key to a great tour? Impact. Tours that focus on facts alone will not inspire anyone. Tours that open a donor's eyes to impact or engage them in an experience will generate the highest philanthropic response.

What's the difference? On a hospital tour, for example, the tour leader wouldn't say, "Here's our physical therapy room." Instead, he or she might say, "Here's where children who have experienced head trauma relearn to walk." Each stop on the tour focuses on the impact of the activity that happens there. With each segment, the tour leader is helping donors visualize and build an emotional connection to the outcome of the work. During a well-conducted tour, donors should exclaim, "I had no idea!" many times while commenting on the amazing impact of your organization.

A virtual tour. Here, again, is an idea born out of necessity. During the coronavirus outbreak, people were not able to come and tour in person. But we didn't let that stop our clients. We helped them combine photos, videos, and talking points into virtual tours. This idea will live for a long time, and I think it has a role in future fundraising. It's especially helpful if distance, age, or physical disabilities are factors with a donor. Virtual tours engage people who head to a warmer climate for the winter, or who spend their summers at a lake house far from home. They serve the same purpose as an in-person tour, but provide far more reach and flexibility.

Access to the CEO. As I mentioned earlier in this chapter, the CEO or Executive Director can inspire donors in many ways. A well organized breakfast, lunch, or dinner with the CEO packs a powerful punch and provides the donor with the inside scoop on the strategic direction of your organization. Plus, from an efficiency point of view, a meal with the CEO yields a high ratio of emotion to time, both for the donor and the leader.

Mission-based participant activities. Think about the programs offered by your organization. How can donors experience your mission through those programs? The hospital I mentioned earlier, for example, invites donors to take part in adaptive sports programs. Those donors experience firsthand the personal and physical strength required to adapt their favorite sports to a disability that can come after an illness or injury. The donors are also inspired by the people they meet and the stories they hear. The nice thing about a donor event that involves existing programs is that the activities sell themselves! And since the program already exists, the development cost is minimal to nonexistent.

Small group cultivation events. Small group events create high impact. They also provide great flexibility when it comes to location. We have seen organizations schedule small group cabarets and ensembles for performing arts organizations, and wild flower tours at a nature center. Other organizations have scheduled bike rides and golf cart tours on trails, dinners in barns, and many other cultivation events that help connect donors directly to the mission. Your organization does not need to overproduce an event in a jaw-dropping venue to experience success. The key is to invite people who will care about the mission, and allow them to experience that mission in an intimate space. Then the location becomes less important, and the message becomes more so.

Major gifts program. A well-defined major gifts structure helps donors understand the impact of their philanthropy. When giving levels are connected to something tangible, donors can appreciate how their gift contributes to your organization's mission. For example, the hospital's major gift program shows donors that $1,500 covers the cost of one inpatient night. A gift of $2,500 pays for a piece of medical equipment. If a donor gets really excited about a particular portion of the mission, he or she might be inclined to give more once it's clear how much investment is required to make that program or service happen. Remember that major gift levels should align with the current giving levels of donors in the database. The top tier should stretch the top donors. A small organization might start with a giving level of $500, with the highest gift at $5,000. A large organization with a more mature donor base might start at $1,000, with the highest levels reaching $25,000, $50,000, or more. More levels can be added as the size of the donor gifts grows. When this structured program is combined with customized cultivation plans, donors naturally "climb the ladder." Eventually, they become ready for more significant requests when your organization has capital or endowment needs.

Video. This is the one tool on my list that might require a larger financial investment. However, I have a growing appreciation for an excellent video edited to multiple lengths. Videos are great door openers. A 3-minute video embedded in an email or social media post captures the heart of your organization's mission through the voices of clients, volunteers, and leaders. And since technology is ultra-portable, a video can be shown almost anywhere. Videos work well in one-on-one meetings because they help orient donors very quickly to the mission and impact of your organization. An excellent video shown to a large group creates buzz! It also builds appreciation for the impact your organization has on the people it serves. And again, a video works wonders at a virtual event, or when connecting with a donor who lives far away.

Additional Examples of Mission-Based Participant Activities

The most difficult tool to develop can be the one that engages donors in the actual work of your organization's mission. For some organizations, existing program activities can easily be adapted to include donors. But for other organizations, the work is a little harder.

The challenge is to find something unusual or exclusive that will deepen the donor's personal connection to the mission. On the flip side, it shouldn't be contrived. Remember that the goal is to bring people closer to who and what your organization is. Here's the good news: I have yet to find an organization that couldn't dream up something effective once they worked on it!

Here are a few more examples of small group cultivation events from nonprofit organizations of all different kinds. Each one found a creative way to draw donors more deeply into their mission.

- **A social work agency**. Due to confidentiality issues, this group cannot bring donors along when volunteers meet with underage clients. That means their regular programs are not open to donors. However, those donors can come to public events where they see volunteers in action. They can come to the swearing in ceremony, where the volunteers commit to doing what's best for each child. Those are powerful, emotional experiences that help donors understand the gravity and impact of the organization's role.
- **A performing arts organization**. These folks were performing a musical. So they invited small groups of donors to dinner in a rehearsal space before the show. Several cast members then spoke with the group before the show, talking about their characters and even giving pointers about what to watch for during the production. The donors loved hearing the stories

from the cast members and getting to know the actors personally.

- **A community foundation**. This organization invests in projects such as trails and parks for the good of the local community. They threw a themed party at an iconic location, complete with a local chef and a meat smoker. They also brought in a historian who captured people's imaginations with the local history. These lucky folks were also invited on an exclusive tour inside a piece of historic architecture.
- **A faith-based ministry**. This organization provides material support and educational opportunities for its local community. They invited donors to come work in the food pantry for a few hours. Donors met the clients, heard their stories, and gained firsthand knowledge about the challenging life circumstances faced by many people in the neighborhood. They also heard about the hope that this organization provides through its services.
- **A senior living facility**. This organization provides a continuum of senior living facilities, from independent living all the way up to full-time nursing. They also offer memory loss care. In order to help donors understand what it's like to lose functionality with age, they pulled out a special suit that they use during staff training. The hands of that suit are stiff, making it hard to do simple tasks like putting on socks or opening a jar. It has weighted feet, which make walking and balancing very difficult. Donors gained instant empathy for the struggles seniors face as they age.
- **A dedicated foundation**. This nonprofit raises money to invest in educational resources that exceed the school's per-pupil stipend from the state. At this event, teachers explained how they use interactive whiteboards and clickers to increase student

engagement. The donors experienced this hands-on, reviewing the projects the foundation had funded in the past year and using the tools to participate in the discussion. They realized that they were paying a lot more attention when they had the chance to participate regularly.

From the Toolshed

Still not sure about how to use existing resources and stock the wheelbarrow with compelling experiences? Here's a great way to gain some insight into what may get donors excited about your organization's mission.

When I'm doing training with board members or fundraising volunteers, I often ask the attendees to identify the nonprofit organization to which they are most cultivated (outside of their faith organization and the one that brought them to the training). Then I ask them how they became so closely connected to that particular organization.

I get wildly divergent answers to that question! Responses include things like this:

"I volunteered for Hospice and saw firsthand how they impacted people at their most vulnerable time…at the end of life."

"My friend invited me to an event. I heard the stories and now I'm hooked."

"My so-and-so (brother, parent, etc.) was impacted by this organization. This is personal for our family."

No one — repeat, no one — says they were cultivated through an annual appeal or newsletter. Don't get me wrong…these are important ways to nourish donor relationships. Think of them as rain. Every plant in the garden can probably use some rain. However, rain alone will not yield the biggest, most beautiful blooms.

So if you're struggling to create experiences that connect donors to your organization's mission, do a little research. The most accessible audience for that research is board members, donors, and volunteers.

Organize a few small groups of 5-10 people, and ask the same question that I ask. Find out how they got interested in other organizations.

Make sure to ask how they became interested in your organization! This will provide ideas about what matters to your organization's donors. That information, in turn, will inspire creative, compelling activities scaled to your organization's capabilities.

FIVE: BUILD A HIVE

"The bee is more honored than other animals, not because she labors, but because she labors for others."

— St. John Chrysostom, Archbishop of Constantinople

I'm fortunate to have a fabulous garden in front of my home. I would love to tell you that it is the result of my own labor. In truth, our condo association works with a superb landscape architect. I spend a lot of time on my front porch, observing the growth in the garden. It starts out quietly in early spring, when it is little more than sticks and mulch, then crescendos into a grand symphony that blooms from June to October. Each of the flowers and plants has a part to play, and a time to play that part. It is remarkable in every way.

When I am truly present and observant, what first catches my eye is the daily progress of our snowball hydrangeas. They start out as simple brown stems and grow into massive snowball flowers. By September, they have succumbed to their own weight and fallen over. I also notice the bursts of color from the perennials, expertly orchestrated around the annuals. Then I notice the chirping of the birds and the differing trills of the songbirds. If I'm lucky, I might glimpse a butterfly during the day. In the evening, I might even catch sight of a bat. The last thing I usually notice is the humming of the bees. Ahh…the bees.

It's true that the gardener plays a critical role in the garden. But without the bees, most flowers won't pollinate and reproduce. Those busy bees flit from flower to flower, collecting and transferring pollen. The bees are absolutely essential to perpetuating the gorgeous plants that make us ooh and aah through the summer and right into the fall. The gardener can't do the work of a bee! But he or she trusts that the bees will be there and do their work.

At this point in our book, it would be natural to feel overwhelmed. I'm sure it's becoming clear that a more successful philanthropic model relies on developing customized cultivation pathways for individual donors. This is on top of the work already being done by people who don't have any more capacity. I hope I am making the case that the time invested in these strategies is well worth the return on investment. They are not additive. They should *replace* more time-intensive fundraising activities that generate less return on investment.

This is where the gardener can breathe a sigh of relief. Help is on the way. It's time to build a beehive. And who belongs in it? Pollinators.

In his book, "The Tipping Point," Malcolm Gladwell identifies three types of people.[1] I was fascinated by his concept, and ended up interviewing more than a dozen people for this book to understand their roles more fully. My findings led me to christen some of these people as "pollinators" because of their unique behavior.

For the most part, I had observed these pollinators during my fundraising career but I didn't really understand what they were doing. They were always the pensive-looking ones in the room, looking as if they were working to connect the dots in the vast, web-like networks they hold in their heads. It struck me that they were like those bees in the garden, flitting from plant to plant and flower to flower, providing for needs and serving others. One of those pollinators, author Sheila VanZile, explained it to me this way. "I can look at a list all day long and I'll know 10 of the 100 people. But point me at 20 people you want to know, and I'll find a way to get to them. Just tell me what you want to know. If you tell me that people have capacity to give and I don't know them, I'll figure out a way to get to them. There's no such thing as no solution. There's always a path!"

---

[1] Gladwell, Malcolm. *The Tipping Point: How Little Things Can Make a Big Difference.* Little, Brown and Company. 2002.

But here's the challenge. In an actual garden, the gardener can't do all the work. He or she is busy planting new flowers, adjusting the sprinklers, applying the fertilizer, and doing all the other work that needs to be done. Gardeners can't pollinate plants. They don't have time, and they don't have the ability.

The same is true in your organization. In practice, organizations have relied on their staff (Executive Directors or Development Officers) to shoulder the burden of determining how, or even if, the donor community is connected to the mission of the organization. How is it physically possible for the staff to do all the work *and* direct the overall strategy for each donor "flower?" It's really pretty simple. The fundraising staff is most successful as the gardeners, not the bees. This was the big aha I had while observing my garden.

Having more than one pollinator gives your organization the capacity to cultivate exponentially more donors. It also preserves those relationships as staff changes occur.

Let's go back to the idea we've been exploring, that of customized cultivation pathways. In Chapter Four, I explained how to stock the development wheelbarrow with some essential tools. However, I also mentioned that your organization doesn't need to use every tool with each person. In other words, when crafting the customized cultivation pathway for each donor or donor prospect, pick the tools and the sequence that will be most effective based on that donor's interests and needs.

Logically, the first question arising from this statement is something like, "How am I supposed to know what to use with each donor?" This is where pollinators come in. They know people. They've picked up tidbits of useful information about interests, hobbies, families, and a whole lot more. The gardener's job is not to know everything. Instead, his or her job is to build a small Donor Development Committee (a "hive") of pollinators who care about your organization's mission and want to put their knowledge to good use. These people help determine which tools, and in which sequence, should be used with each of your organization's donors or donor prospects. That knowledge will help cultivate prospects to their maximum potential gift.

~ An Illustration ~

Sheila helped me with the question of what makes pollinators tick. I asked her why she helped people connect with other people who met their needs. She said, "I think curiosity has a lot to do with it. I've spent my lifetime trying to engage with people and make them feel like they've left with something more than what they came with. I think that's part of that whole pollinator role. Our goal is to enrich someone's life in some way. There is nothing about being a pollinator that is self-serving. For me, it's just the sheer joy of putting it together.

"When I support a nonprofit organization, I want to put my network to use for them. Here's a good example. I was on a committee for a local school, so I planned to attend their gala. We really wanted to get our friends to the event. I knew the husband loved helicopters, and there would be a few on display at the gala. So I invited this couple, and made sure we sat at a table with a well-known local helicopter pilot who is connected to the school's founder. During dinner, that pilot offered to take us all on a helicopter tour above Mackinac Island. We flew all over the place, and then went out to a lovely restaurant. Ultimately, our friends made a very nice gift to the school, and then doubled it after hearing one of the students speak. I knew they would love the school's mission, so I figured out a path to get them engaged based on what I knew about them."

This is really quite profound when you break it down. Sheila knew the donor prospect and had specific information about their interests that could connect them to the school. She used a tool from the school's wheelbarrow (the gala) and strategically placed this donor prospect next to people who shared the prospect's outside interests but were also passionate about the school. Ultimately, they made a significant gift. The school incurred no additional costs. Sheila used their existing resources well. And what was in it for Sheila? The "psychic income" that comes with knowing her action has yielded a good result.

The Lesson: Nonprofit organizations often undervalue pollinators because they are not usually the ones with the most obvious resources. In fact, pollinators purposely run under the radar. However, their natural skill at bringing people together is priceless. They get great joy from finding a path and helping people solve problems. Pollinators will provide your organization with insider information about how to engage donors with the mission. In doing so, they will help your organization raise more money!

~

Stock Up on Pollinators

I've seen pollinators work their magic time and time again. The pollinator flips through his or her mental Rolodex and starts buzzing with ideas. "I know this person, here's what she can do for your organization. In fact, we'll get together for coffee and talk about this, this, and this." The same is true for the next person on the list. "Okay, that guy is a professor at the local college. I think he's also made some money because he's written some excellent textbooks that have sold really well. Here's how he could help, and here's how we get him engaged."

Pollinators can do this work because they are curious about others, and they retain bits of information about everyone they meet. Think again about the bees. A bee's tiny little feet land on a flower and pick up a bit of pollen. As that bee keeps buzzing from place to place, it picks up pollen everywhere! Pollinators gather up information by asking questions. Sheila says, "Everybody has something unique.

You don't always find it the first time you meet them. If you're curious enough and get people talking, you find out that they're in some kind of crazy car collector club or that they love to go to Tucson four times a year, or something like that." That curiosity, coupled with intentionality about remembering and then recalling information, is what makes pollinators so effective.

A Donor Development Committee is an essential resource as your organization starts developing customized cultivation pathways. I recommend that you find 4-8 pollinators who can help identify the right steps to take with each person on the donor or donor prospect list.

The logical question is, "Where do pollinators come from?" Let's start by analyzing the board. A board typically includes three types of people.

Mavens are subject experts. They're influential due to some combination of knowledge, experience, and wealth.

Salespeople gain influence by their ability to persuade. Generally, they will do anything they're asked to do. They won't necessarily be able to come up with a plan, but they can execute.

Pollinators are those who draw from personal knowledge to intuitively understand how they can reach people and engage them in the mission.

Imagine every bad joke you've ever heard that starts out, "Three people walk into a bar." Now think of that joke in the context of mavens, salespeople, and pollinators. Imagine the conversation in the room if a few people are talking about donor cultivation. The question on the table is, "How can we engage prospective donor X in our work?"

The maven will say, "I know that person." And that's as far as his or her contribution goes. The maven has knowledge, but may not knit it together to go any further.

The salesperson will say, "If you get me the appointment, I can make the ask." The salesperson is fearless, but doesn't always know how to navigate the space between where the relationship is now and where it needs to be in order to garner a large gift.

The pollinator will say, "I know that X is interested in such-and-such. Y is also interested in that, and I know she would be willing to make an introduction. I'll ask her to set it up." The pollinator draws from a deep well of knowledge to bring the right people and steps together in the cultivation process.

How would you assess your organization's board? A typical board has mostly mavens, a couple of salespeople, and few, if any, pollinators.

While writing this book, I reviewed more than 75 board assessments that my consulting firm had conducted over nearly 15 years. That research confirmed what I suspected. Most nonprofit boards are made up of 75-80% mavens and only 20% salespeople. These organizations had few, if any, pollinators.

But the pollinators are the ones your organization needs to be more successful in fundraising. Specifically, they need to be on the Donor Development Committee. They have a vast pool of knowledge and an innate ability to pull information together into a logical plan.

That's why it's important to include non-board members in the Donor Development Committee, especially if your organization's board is a little thin in the pollinator department or if the board has a prescribed composition. This is a great way to expand your organization's volunteer base and recruit for a specific purpose. I can't stress enough how important this is. Without the right people, the Donor Development Committee won't successfully help with the work.

This is why it matters. In our earlier examples, notice the pollinator isn't just saying, "I know this person." That's what a maven would say. The pollinator takes it further. "I know this person. Here's how he or she could become engaged to help." That's pollinating at its finest.

True pollinators have exactly the right skill set, and they love to do the work! Sheila VanZile notes, "Why wouldn't I use all of this energy that I have invested for the last fifteen years for something else other than just the conversations I've had? It would seem to me like a crime not to use that knowledge. There is an incredible sense of satisfaction to know that you can help people solve problems in a much more simple way."

I do have one word of caution. Watch out for artificial pollinators! These are people who will get to know others and keep contact information, but it's for personal gain. True pollinators are genuine, according to Sheila. "When I meet people, I'm not looking for anything. I just have this desire to help. If I know someone who fits the bill, I connect them. I get real joy out of saying, 'You need this, and I know a person who can help you.'"

From the Toolshed

So now it's time to find those pollinating bees. They're essential to your organization's success in building customized cultivation pathways for donors.

The logical question is, "How can we find them?" Think about the donors and volunteers connected to your organization. Look for people who exhibit these kinds of character traits:

- Always heard saying, "You should talk to so-and-so"
- Seem to have a mental Rolodex of people, their hobbies, and interests
- Exhibit genuine curiosity about others and will spend time getting to know new people
- Always keep the contact information of people they've met
- Have passion for and a deeply personal connection to your organization's cause
- Active and well-connected on social media
- Want to help solve problems

- Often willing to mentor others

A simple score sheet might help. List potential bees along the left, and across the top, list the attributes of a pollinator. Ask a few trusted people to help evaluate each person according to those attributes. Trust me…the pollinators will stand out!

SIX: START POLLINATING!

"Buckminster Fuller himself was fond of stating what seems to be happening at the moment is never the full story of what is really going on. He liked to point out that for the honey bee, it is the honey that is important. But the bee is at the same time nature's vehicle for carrying out cross-pollination of the flowers. Interconnectedness is a fundamental principal of nature. Each event connects with others."

— Jon Kabat-Zinn, Professor Emeritus, University of Massachusetts Medical School

I want to take just a moment at this point in the book to reflect back. Do you remember reading in the Introduction that this approach to philanthropy might seem counterintuitive and even slow? If you've made it to this point, you're probably wondering, "When does the organization actually start raising money?"

This approach requires a planned ramp-up and preparation process. That, too, is consistent with our gardening metaphor. Successful gardeners know that preparation matters. They don't spontaneously buy plants at a greenhouse sale and plop them in the ground. No, serious gardeners take time. They design. They plan. They meticulously till the soil, adding the proper nutrients and compost to create optimal soil conditions. They buy the tools and purchase the plants. Then, and only then, are they ready to put seedlings into the ground. The preparation is worth it, however, when the flowers burst into bloom and the amazing garden takes shape. After all that time, suddenly the beauty pops into view, seemingly overnight!

The same is true for customized cultivation pathways. It can take quite a while to do all the prep work outlined in the previous chapters. But once the planning is complete, the fun begins! This is where your organization starts leveraging the knowledge of the Donor Development Committee to build stronger relationships with the targeted list of donors. That's the work that leads to larger and more consistent gifts. So in this chapter, I'm going to show you how to get those pollinator bees busy in the donor garden.

Start by gathering information. Your pollinators will intuitively gather information and link people to each other. The Donor Development Committee needs to pick their brains for every nugget of information about the identified donor prospects.

The first step is a massive information download. Gather the Donor Development Committee together. Give them the list of prospects, and start going through it donor by donor. Learn about each prospect's personal story and gain an understanding about how they are connected to the organization's mission. Take detailed notes. This process allows pollinators to share what they know about each person's motivations and passions. These conversations will yield a lot of information, because pollinators are curious and they remember. Depending on the length of the prospect list, this work could take a few meetings. What should emerge is a fairly comprehensive picture of what motivates each donor.

The second step is to go back to the top of the list and map out a customized cultivation pathway for each donor. I always like to have three action steps identified in each pathway so that I know what needs to happen next. I find a grid is the easiest way to map things out. Along the left, list the donor prospect names. Along the top, note the tools in the wheelbarrow based on the work from Chapter 4. (This could include things like a tour, a small group event, or meeting with the Executive Director.) As the Donor Development Committee talks through each prospect, members can decide which tools, and in which order, should be used for that person. Also make sure the members identify the person who is responsible for each step.

The volunteers are essential here. Don't ignore their advice! Their insights are critical in helping to identify the donor's motivations, and pinpointing what might be interesting to them about the organization. Never forget that different people can be interested in the same organization for wildly divergent reasons. It's important to understand those motivations in order to build inclination. That's the whole point of this book.

And here's another critical point: don't let anything stand in the way of moving forward. Some of our clients wanted to back off on donor cultivation during the pandemic. They were afraid people would not want to talk to them. In fact, the opposite was true! In many cases, people were craving connections with others. So we put the power of video conferencing to work and helped clients prepare talking points they could use for virtual rather than in-person meetings. The results were amazing. In another one of those counterintuitive circumstances, people actually had *more time* to talk because they were unable to do many of their routine activities. They wanted to know how the organizations they cared about were surviving and moving forward. This drove home the point one more time for me: don't assume! Engaged donors respond to their favorite organizations, regardless of world circumstances.

~ An Illustration ~

I happen to love plays and musicals. I'm very fond of a theatre group and I wanted to help bring some new donors into their garden. So in this case, I was a volunteer on the Donor Development Committee. I recommended a backstage tour for two prospective donors, but for different reasons.

One of my friends, Sue, was an artist. She had done some set design for the local high school while she worked there. I knew the process fascinated her, so I arranged a backstage pass during the performance of *A Christmas Story*. She saw firsthand how a complicated set like this worked, and she also talked shop with the set designers. It was right up her alley!

Another friend, Linda, loves musicals. What musical could be more epic than *Les Miserables*? We also ventured backstage before this show. This time, however, the focus was on the music itself, and what to look for at key points during the performance. She, too, ate this up.

We used the same tool — in this case, a backstage visit — for two people to become further engaged with the same organization. However, we placed a completely different emphasis on each visit, aligning our speakers and content to the donor's individual motivations. Both people became more cultivated, but for different reasons. At the same time, the passionate staff and volunteers had the opportunity to connect with donors in meaningful and authentic ways. They're excited to help, too!

The Lesson: A nonprofit organization has many facets. Donors will be attracted to different aspects of an organization based on their own personal motivations and experiences. It is essential to understand and connect to each donor's motivation in order to increase their inclination — and eventually their gifts — to the organization.

~

Success Hinges on Pollinators

I need to reiterate the importance of pollinators in this work. (If you're a little fuzzy about who and what pollinators are, make sure you go back and re-read Chapter Five.) Pollinators gather and retain information about people. It's just the way their brains are wired. They're also naturally curious and they ask a lot of questions. Ultimately, they build relationships with people who share their interests and passions.

Pollinators know a lot, and they know a lot of people. But perhaps more importantly, pollinators understand what motivates people. They can intuitively take a fact ("Jane loves music"), understand the motivation behind that fact ("She wasn't good at sports in school, but she loved to play the piano"), and connect it to a cause ("I think Jane would be really interested in bringing music to elementary school kids"). And because they understand how facts connect to motivations, pollinators can help you create a customized cultivation pathway that draws each donor prospect closer to the work of your organization.

Many of us have heard the expression, "Everything looks like a nail when the only tool you have is a hammer." That's often a disturbingly accurate analogy for traditional fundraising. Everyone gets a newsletter. Everyone gets an annual appeal. And it would be tempting, once the wheelbarrow is filled with tools, to start using all of them with everyone. I've seen organizations do just that. Please, don't do it!

I can't stress enough that pollinators should help drive the strategy with each person. Figure out the best combination of tools, in the best order, for each person. Take that marvelous intuition that pollinators bring to the table and leverage it. Pollinators understand what motivates people. Laurie, another pollinator I interviewed, puts it this way. "I think one of the important aspects of connecting is to bring out that emotional element; to listen to why the donor is excited, what their story is or was, to give them that platform to speak from as well as to encourage it and provide more information."

Using that knowledge to create the right sequence of activities will yield the most cultivated donors and the largest possible gifts. Remember our equation:

Resources + Inclination = The Gift

Here's another important thing to remember. Donors who have been individually cultivated *want to make a larger gift*. By step three in the cultivation pathway, they're excited about your organization's mission. They're personally connected to it. Through giving, the donor gets the opportunity to do something that is deeply meaningful to him or her.

When Donors Start Self-Pollinating

That can lead to another fascinating phenomenon that feels wildly counterintuitive. Fully cultivated donors start volunteering their time and personal resources to further the mission of organizations *without being asked*!

Don't believe it can actually happen? Let me share a story from my personal experience.

I am deeply connected to the Girls Choral Academy in Grand Rapids, Michigan. Their mission is to develop self-confidence in girls through participation in choral music. Having spent 12 years in choir myself, I connect deeply to that mission. Back in 2005, I was idly watching a Food Network special at home one night. It featured a phenomenal all-female band, The Biddies, playing on the sidewalk during the intro to the show. Intrigued, I checked out their website. These young women were very experienced and competent musicians. This "cocktail pop band" was part of the Carnegie Hall outreach program. Carnegie Hall actually paid them to bring music into the community.

Conveniently enough, The Biddies' website offered a calendar of engagements. So next time I was in New York City, I hopped on the subway and headed out to Queens District Library to hear them live, just like a regular groupie! We chatted after the performance, and I started asking what it would take to get them to Grand Rapids.

The Biddies were receptive to the idea of a Midwest visit. More importantly, the leadership at Girls Choral Academy was willing to indulge me. My desire to bring in a professional band to sing with the girls aligned perfectly with their mission to build girls' self esteem.

I teamed up with two friends and we brought The Biddies to Grand Rapids. They headlined a benefit concert for Girls Choral Academy, singing on their own as well as with the girls in the choir. The girls were head-over-heels excited to be singing with a real band! My friends and I were even more excited, because we produced the whole show. We had a stage full of girls up there, singing their hearts out with The Biddies! Believe me, this experience gave me more pleasure than it gave them.

Over the years, I had the opportunity to reprise that original opportunity with the Girls Choral Academy and showcase The Biddies at different kid-friendly venues around town. In the process, I pushed myself to expand my own capabilities. I was able to express my passion for mentorship. I put my heart, soul, and wallet into these concerts to reach girls all over the city. Am I fully cultivated with Girls Choral Academy? You bet I am! I can't believe we made this all happen. And I will always be grateful to them for letting me do it.

This is the kind of mutually fulfilling and deeply rewarding relationship that pollinators can help your organization develop. Tapping into a donor's personal passions yields amazing results. This approach produces a simply stunning donor garden!

From the Toolshed

I'm not a big forms person. But this is one part of my work where forms are absolutely essential. I use the Cultivation Worksheet all the time to keep track of customized cultivation pathways. Let's map one out.

To begin, set up a spreadsheet or make a document with columns.

First we're going to work across the top. Starting with the second column, enter a label at the top of each one. That label represents one of the tools in your organization's wheelbarrow. So the columns might be labeled "Tour," "Lunch w/ CEO," "Invite to gala," etc.

Now we're going to work down the left side. In the second row, put the name of the first donor prospect. Then move to the next row and enter another one, and so forth.

When the form is complete, it will show a grid of people and potential donor-driven activities.

At the next Donor Development Committee meeting, talk through each donor and identify the three steps that should be taken with that person. Working across that person's row, put a 1 in the box that aligns with the first step, and note behind it who is responsible for that step. Then put a 2 in the box of the next step, along with a name. Do the same with 3.

Here's a very small sample of what a first line might look like.

Sample Cultivation Worksheet

	Exhibition	Gala	Tour	Lunch w/ CEO	Client Program
Jane Smith		3 (Jeff)	2 (Susan)		1 (Bill)

As the Development Committee works through the steps, put check marks in the boxes to show what has been completed. This tool provides an at-a-glance way to keep track of all cultivation activities. Working through this list should be part of every Donor Development Committee meeting.

And then don't forget the last, but certainly important, step: put this information in the donor database. This is the organization's central record of what has happened with each donor. That information should be available to support your organization's long-term fundraising success.

Seven: Keep the Bees Happy!

"The little bee returns with evening's gloom, to join her comrades in the braided hive, where, housed beside their mighty honey-comb, they dream their polity shall long survive."

— Charles Tennyson Turner, English Poet

Many gardeners will tell you that they select certain plants for the garden based on their function. For example, they might choose species that attract butterflies, or pay particular attention to hummingbird favorites. On the other end of the spectrum is a gardener fully committed to marigolds that will keep the pesky deer out of the more desirable plants.

But one thing you probably won't see is a gardener who tries to prevent bees from spending time in the garden. Bees are essential. And I like to think that happy bees…those that have many flowers to buzz around without being swatted away…make sweeter honey. (No science here, mind you, just a personal belief!)

Pollinators need to be happy in order to do their best work. When they are happy, they create pathways to successful fundraising.

As mentioned in an earlier chapter, I had a chance to talk with many pollinators as this book took shape. It was fascinating to hear how these very different people all repeated the same themes about why they do what they do. Equally fascinating were the conversations about what would shut down or redirect their enthusiasm.

Your organization needs to be really good at beekeeping in order to succeed with personalized cultivation pathways. When the environment keeps these pollinators buzzing around, your organization will see fantastic results.

Here are a few of the important things I learned from the bees themselves about how to keep them engaged.

Understand why they care about your organization. Take time to sit down with each one. Understand his or her story. Genuine interest matters. (They're connecting with *you* at this point!)

Get them personally involved with the donors they know. Pollinators are most useful when they leverage their personal knowledge about a particular person. They can help plan strategies, but they can also extend invitations and help with the thank-you. They are integral to the entire cultivation process and they enjoy it.

Follow their lead. These bees know their stuff! That's why they're on the Donor Development Committee. Listen to their insights about donor motivations, and use their guidance to create the right cultivation pathway for each person. This may be hard, especially if their recommendations don't align with what the organization might have done if left to its own devices. Remember that they have the organization's best interests at heart, and they probably know the donor prospects best.

Don't start until your tools are ready. Don't engage pollinators until all the preparation work is done and it's time to begin implementing the steps they recommend. Try moving a few personal donor connections through the process before engaging the pollinators, so their connections can be top priority later. Pollinators are fast-paced people, and they need others to keep up!

Keep them posted on outcomes. Pollinators need to know they are valued and that your organization is using their knowledge and efforts. Make sure to let them know how their suggestions worked out.

Thank them in a way that's meaningful to each one. This is an important lesson. Some pollinators love a personal note. Others don't want to be thanked at all…they just want to do their thing. It's important to understand the pollinators as thoroughly as the donors.

Remember that this is their gift. I mentioned in Chapter Five that, although pollinators can be found in every socio-economic group, they are not always the wealthiest members of the community. They are giving their time and talent to your organization, and it is as precious as someone else's treasure. Be sure to value it highly!

On the flip side, you want to avoid behaviors that will send these valuable pollinator bees buzzing off to do their good work in another place. Bees will not keep trying to pollinate plastic flowers, for example, because they know there's no reward for their effort. The same is true for fundraising pollinators. They may love your organization, but they're not going to keep investing time and energy if their efforts do not pay off. Remember: they gain their psychic income from successfully completing their role and advancing the mission. If they don't see results and feel successful, they're not making that income.

What are some of the things to avoid?

Don't ignore their suggestions. These people are on the Donor Development Committee precisely because of their connections. Don't ask them to help create a donor strategy and then ignore their advice, especially if they know the donor well and your organization does not.

Don't waste the connections. Pollinators are very selective about who they put into their mental Rolodex. If they attempt to make a connection and there's no follow up from the organization, that's a poor reflection on them. Do that two or three times, and they simply won't listen the next time they are asked to help.

Don't undervalue their work. It's easy to gush about big donor gifts, and your organization obviously should be very appreciative of them. But think about this: without pollinators, there probably wouldn't have been a strong relationship that led to the gift! The pollinator's work is literally priceless. Make sure they know how much they are valued and appreciated.

There is a caveat with all this. Beekeeping is important work, because it's going to help your organization build those customized cultivation pathways that ultimately lead to the largest gifts. And while the bees are very welcome, they should not take charge of your organization's fundraising efforts. The gardener is still the gardener!

What's the difference? Let's think of it in gardening terms again. A gardener can't create a beautiful design if all he or she focuses on is the needs of the bees. And the bees, quite frankly, can't create a holistic garden design on their own. They don't have the perspective or the knowledge of the whole plan. If it were up to the bees, for example, there probably wouldn't be any nonflowering green plants in the garden! But the gardener knows those plants create visual diversity and amazing texture. He or she incorporates green plants, flowering shrubs, architectural elements, and art to create a beautiful whole. And while the bees will focus their buzzing activity on the flowers, that doesn't mean the other parts of the garden are any less essential to the overall impact of the garden.

It's important to understand and communicate with the pollinator bees so they understand their role. Listen to their counsel in developing customized cultivation pathways for the people they know. But their other ideas for philanthropy, or even for your mission and programs, are just that...ideas. These things are the equivalent of architectural elements or garden art. The bees are not responsible for them! Pollinators may not be board members. And they are not usually on the leadership team.

This can be a tricky balance to achieve. As pollinator relationships grow stronger, channel that enthusiasm in ways that benefit your organization. It's important to understand the difference between ideas to help cultivate donors vs. ideas about the organization. I heard one client summarize it pretty succinctly. "Sometimes I get three or four calls per day from the same person," she said. "They get so much psychic income from connecting that they want me to go along with every bright idea. I've become friends with many of them and I'm getting more comfortable saying, 'No' or explaining why we are not moving forward with their ideas."

~ An Illustration ~

As I was talking to people about this book, I had a chance to connect with one of my local "bee friends." (Let's call him Jack.)

I've known Jack for many years, and I've watched him leverage his connections time and time again for organizations that matter to him. So I asked him, "Jack, why do you do this work?"

Jack's answer shines a light on several things we've highlighted in this chapter. "Well," he said, "The first thing is that I don't do it for recognition. Some people like to be in the spotlight, but not me. I like the networking, and I like to see the results. That's the ROI for me."

But then he went on to highlight something that every gardener should hear. "I never know what happens when I make a connection," he observed rather wistfully. "Did it work? Did they follow through? It would be really helpful for me to know how it worked out. In fact, I would send a thank-you to the person if I knew that they had responded. And yeah, that kind of feedback would be pretty motivating for me too!"

Jack was equally clear about the things that take away his motivation. "I've been part of organizations that ask for my help but don't follow through," he notes. "One, in particular, I've just removed myself from because they don't want to interact with the people who could help them! They want a free ride but won't do the work to follow up on what I've offered. And then I'm done."

The Lesson: Pollinators are going to generate work! They will always create tasks for follow-up. Make sure to follow through, because the work will lead to good things. If there's no follow through, the bees will find another garden to pollinate.

~

What's in It for Them?

Let's understand a little more about what motivates pollinator bees. Why do they do what they do? The motivations may vary somewhat, but essentially, it comes down to altruism. Pollinators do what they do because it makes them happy. They're not connecting for personal or professional gain. It's simply how they are wired.

What are some of the primary rewards for these bees? Here are quotes from a few with whom I've worked over the years.

Personal satisfaction. "I try to gain whatever knowledge I can in the relationship-building area. When I see people that 'fit' with each other or who can help someone else, I connect them, especially when introductions will enable pathways. What makes people happy? What helps people be the best they can be? That's the philosophy I live with. And I love people! Nothing makes me happier than to connect with others when I see a fit or an opportunity to support."

Furthering an organization's mission. "For me, the natural part of this comes from my heart, because it's aligned to the mission. I start there because that's where everything else comes from if you care about what you're doing. Identifying an emotional connection is really important because it gives people an opportunity to share their story. If I can generate enthusiasm for the cause, that's all I need. I don't need somebody to say, 'Oh you're the best person at this work in town.' And I don't need to be at events where my face is out there. That's just not me."

An opportunity to help. "When I hear someone talk, I instantly go to, 'Who do I know that knows how to do that?' or 'Who do I know that's in that?' Instantly. It's almost like a Rolodex in my head. I think part of me is also a fixer. I want to help, even if the person is not asking for help! It feels like an accomplishment when I see two different ends that I could bring together. It makes me feel like I've helped someone."

A sense of purpose. "Many people are looking for happiness. I see it every day in people I know. Sometimes I want to shake them and say, 'Stop looking at your therapist! Stop thinking that if you could just buy this, or have this different husband, or do that, you'd be happy.' It's all about giving back to other people and meeting needs. I have found my purpose and my meaning in life by helping to make other people's lives more meaningful."

From the Toolshed

One thing that distinguishes pollinators is their endless fascination with other people. They like to ask questions! And they're good at it, too.

Inquisitiveness can be learned, and it's a trait of all good fundraising professionals. Good listeners excel at relating to everyone they meet. We can all learn something from the bees!

Here's the interesting thing: not all questions are created equal. I find that open-ended questions are far better for learning than closed-ended questions.

What's the difference? A closed-ended question is one that pre-supposes an answer. It might be a yes/no answer, or a "how many" kind of answer. An open-ended question, on the other hand, leaves the answer options completely open. For example, if you are trying to learn about someone's hobbies, you might ask, "Do you like music?" That's a yes/no answer; a closed-ended question. It certainly doesn't give you any indication of where to take the conversation next if the answer is no! What happens if the question is, "What kinds of arts and cultural events do you enjoy?" Regardless of the answer, there's a path to follow as you learn more about the person.

Think about how you personally engage with new people. Do you have a list of questions? Are they open-ended or closed? Open-ended questions will take more time. However, you will go further, faster in the relationship-building process when you allow people to share their personal story through your questions.

Here's a good exercise. Make a list of 3-5 open-ended questions that you think would be good to have ready for new donor meetings, for example. Then find a friendly board member, donor, or volunteer and ask those questions.

If the questions elicit something new about him or her, then congratulations! The questions passed their trial run and also yielded some new information.

If those questions didn't surface any new information, revise them a bit. Go back and examine them carefully. Did they contain some assumptions or presuppositions? Were they truly open-ended questions? Were they too shallow, or did they not get into anything personal? Questioning is an art form. People who can ask good questions excel at building good relationships. Revise the questions and try again! A little practice with open-ended questions makes it much easier to learn about anyone, including donors and pollinators.

EIGHT: FIND JOY IN THE WORK

> *"There can be no other occupation like gardening in which, if you were to creep up behind someone at their work, you would find them smiling."*
>
> — Mirabel Osler, English Writer and Garden Designer

Do you enjoy fundraising?

More than 80% of professional fundraisers report that they are satisfied with many key aspects of their current job, yet half are likely to leave their position within 18 months. This according to a survey by the Association of Fundraising Professionals (AFP) and *The Chronicle of Philanthropy* conducted independently online by the Harris Poll.

How can someone be so passionate about an organization on the one hand, and yet so uncertain that they'll stay? According to this same poll, there's a lot of tension and pressure in most fundraising jobs. Eighty-four percent of participants feel tremendous pressure to succeed in their role.

There's no doubt that philanthropy is hard work. I know this from my personal experience. But here's something I also know:

When organizations move from transactional fundraising to relational fundraising, they rediscover the joy of philanthropy.

This entire book is about bringing the joy back to philanthropy…for the professionals doing the work, the boards and volunteers that support them, and the donors doing the giving. We're going to hear from the donors themselves — the flowers — a bit later in this chapter. But right now, I want to focus on how customized cultivation pathways will help fundraising professionals.

~ An Illustration ~

I know of a social outreach organization that was pretty good at growing donor daisies. They did a dinner. They sent out appeal letters. They wrote some grants. In a nutshell, they were doing transactional fundraising.

A new Executive Director (we will call her Melanie) moved into the Executive Director position in 2005. Shortly after that, the recession of 2008 struck. We started working together and she understood how customized cultivation pathways could work. This completely energized her! The Executive Director is a people person, and this approach resonated with her.

She followed the whole procedure. She created entry points for donors. She formed a Donor Development Committee and prioritized the best potential donors. She made a plan to cultivate each one individually. As we pulled the pieces together, she kept saying, "I can't wait to take this out for a spin!"

When the day finally arrived and she was ready to implement, the results exceeded even her optimistic anticipation. She saw larger gifts after her first tour! That got her revved up about her work. She got her hands dirty in the garden, so to speak, and her plants responded. The organization significantly increased individual giving, and increased their budget from $800,000 to $1.6 million from 2008-2012.

Melanie says, "As a new Executive Director, I was a little overwhelmed with being responsible for fundraising, especially when the economy crashed. Building the plan and taking the steps of individual cultivation was slow going in the beginning. I felt like I needed faster results. But I committed to the plan, and once we began implementing, I saw immediately it was all worth the wait."

The Lesson: Philanthropy is not easy. But customized cultivation pathways are the opposite of a transactional relationship. Your organization is not "selling" something. Instead, there's a personal connection between the donor and your organization's mission. That allows them to find joy in the giving, and professional fundraisers to find joy in the asking.

∼

How Does Life Change for the Gardener?

Gardeners are a passionate group. I don't think I've ever met someone whose garden looks like the cover of a magazine and heard him or her say, "I'm not really interested in the yard. I just garden for something to do." Nope! They will talk my ear off, telling me about this plant and that challenge and the worst case of bugs or blight they ever saw. True gardeners are fanatics in the best sense of the word.

Philanthropy professionals and the teams that support them are passionate, too. So what changes when your organization uses customized cultivation pathways the way I've described them in this book?

Committee members bloom. Be honest for a moment. Do hackles sometimes rise a bit when well-intentioned committees want to plan yet another event? Of course they do!

Here's the problem. The committee members don't really know how to increase donor giving. They're just doing what everyone else does, because it must be right if so many organizations do it! And many of them are probably on the Events Committee because that's the main way that fundraising volunteers engage with nonprofit organizations.

However, when a Donor Development Committee has the right skills and a specific charge, the whole equation changes. I can't say disagreements will disappear. However, I promise that everyone will understand the purpose and the work that needs to be done. This kind of alignment changes everything. Now the Donor Development Committee members are valuable, because they can make those all-important connections. They will bloom, because they have been planted in the place that perfectly fits their talents and personalities.

Donor relationships flourish. Donors give because they find joy in it. The more you can personalize their connection, the more fulfillment they will find in their giving.

It's completely different when donors engage with your organization. Now they experience first-hand the impact of the work. They're excited. They're motivated. More than that, they're on fire for the cause because it aligns with their personal interests. Donors will want to give, because now they understand how their story and interests connect to your organization's work. Donations will grow in an organic way through stronger, more relevant, and personal relationships with the people who care about the mission. They will be known as people, not just as checkbooks.

Gifts grow. This is probably the most important point I can make. When the gardener chooses appropriate plants and then provides the specific care that each one needs, the plants flourish. The same is true with donors. I have never seen any other result in the thirty-plus years I've been doing this work. When donors have a rich, personalized, connected experience, they will give larger gifts. That knowledge alone should help release a little of the pressure. A properly cultivated plant will thrive, and the flower will be there for the picking! That's the fun part…the thing that makes all the work worthwhile.

Yes, it's still work. A donor garden won't grow on its own. But I can promise that this approach yields larger gifts, with longer and better donor relationships. And it's a whole lot more fun to interact with donors personally rather than through the donor database!

How Does Life Change for the Flowers?

We've talked a lot about fundraising from the fundraising professional or the volunteer's point of view. But that's only half of the story. Donor experiences will change as well. A personalized cultivation process changes everything for a donor.

In Chapter Six, I shared some of my own personal experiences with the Girls Choral Academy. They allowed me and my friends to produce an entire show, bringing artists from New York City to Grand Rapids to sing with the girls. I will never, ever forget that experience. The girls made excited exclamations, like, "We just sang with a REAL band," and "That was SO cool" after singing with my friends, The Biddies. I was already very committed to the Girls Choral Academy. However, the experience of working closely with the girls and seeing how profoundly they were impacted sent my dedication to the organization soaring to a new level. I gave to them, but it felt like they gave to me. Now *that* is the ultimate statement from a fully cultivated donor!

This is the rule, rather than the exception. When donors are encouraged to weave deep connections between their personal passions and your organization's mission, their commitment grows exponentially.

I was thankful that our nonprofit clients understood these concepts during the coronavirus pandemic. Donors *wanted* to hear from the organizations they cared about. They wanted the emails, the personal calls, and the letters. They needed to know how organizations were adapting. More importantly, they wanted to know how they could help.

Donors also *wanted to give*. Overall giving during the pandemic started out high for essential services such as food and housing. But donors very quickly understood that they needed to support organizations that were losing huge sources of income, like the performing arts. The organizations that clearly articulated the gap they faced and showed donors how they were staying focused on their mission during the pandemic received overwhelming support. Their donors were not about to let them go under!

Knowing that it's more impactful when a donor speaks for him or her self, let's hear from a few flowers.

"Just Sending Literature Doesn't Do It"

I've worked for many years with a wonderful board member, volunteer, and donor who I'll call John. John is highly cultivated with two particular organizations, and he is pretty clear about why.

"For me, it's about personal experiences. I think that started when I was a child. My dad took me out with him to deliver gifts for the Santa Claus Girls, and my six-year-old self was stunned by how some of the people lived. As I poured out my shock to him after one particular delivery, I remember dad telling me, 'You just had your first lesson in gratitude.' And it's true. As I've interacted with people from the organizations I support, the experiences have humbled me and made me want to do more.

"One of my closest relationships is with an organization that helps men get sober and find employment. The Executive Director calls me occasionally to say thank you. He has invited me for lunch a few times, but we don't go to some fancy restaurant. Nope! We grab plates, go through the line with the men he serves, and then sit down to talk in his office. That simple experience is a great reminder of why I give to them. And the amount of contact is perfect.

"I appreciate leaders who reach out and get to know me as a person. Just sending literature doesn't do it! I'm a face-to-face guy who's dying in this digital world. I want to engage and build a relationship. That relationship doesn't have to be overwhelming or complicated. I'm a simple guy. An occasional phone call or lunch is all I need.

"I'm also deeply passionate about a local camp. That relationship is long and deep, with several generations of my family being very connected through experiences there. But what's most critical to me is that they've stayed true to their mission. So many organizations veer away from their purpose. But for me, consistency matters. I want future generations of my family to have the same character-building experiences and focus that I had, and my parents before me.

That's part of the DNA that connects us to each other and the organization."

"I Want to Be Meat and Potatoes, Not Dessert"

Another one of my longtime relationships is with a generous, warmhearted woman named Michelle. Like John, she is very clear about what matters to her as a donor.

"Consistent, regular communication is key to me. It's not annoying. I want to hear from you! A relationship can't grow unless the parties talk to each other. And since I'm in a relationship with the organizations I support, I want them to tell me how my gift made an impact. In between asks, show me what my gift did. We keep giving to organizations when there is a relationship. If that relationship goes away, the giving will, too.

"It's important for the relationship to be about more than money. I want to use my talents and connections for the organizations I care about. I want to respond to feasibility studies; I want to give advice. I want to volunteer. When an organization values my brain as well as my money, that's really flattering. If they don't, it actually makes me somewhat angry! I want to be the meat and potatoes in a relationship, not just the dessert.

"I've also noticed a tendency for many organizations to brush off female donors. Women drive 75% of the giving in the world. Men are not usually the givers. So be aware that even a gift from a married couple or a family foundation involves individual people who respond to different things. I, for example, don't like to be schmoozed. I love it when you are direct. Make sure you build the relationship around all of the decision makers and what matters to each of them."

"It Needs to Be Personal"

A third person who did me the honor of sharing her perspective is a hardworking volunteer I'll call Ann. She echoed many of the sentiments shared by John and Michelle, but also put her unique viewpoint on being a donor.

"The staff at the organizations I really care about makes the difference. They see and know me as a person. They make me feel important, not just as a donor but as an individual. They get me engaged in projects. They acknowledge and thank me. I feel good when I go there!

"That's important, because I have to be personally involved in the organization to put them on my charitable giving list. I know it's sometimes hard to get in touch with a donor, but not me. As a trustee for our family foundation, I will say, "yes" any time someone asks me to come on a tour. I feel it's my fiduciary responsibility to listen to them and evaluate their work. But if all you do is send a letter and there's no personal contact, forget it! It needs to be personal.

"One of the organizations I hold in high regard is a hospital. After my husband passed away from cancer, I wanted to give back to the hospital because I appreciated the care he had received. I ended up on a cancer committee, and we decided that a Patient Navigator was an essential function to fund. I gave money to hire the first person, and now there are 13 of them! The organization consistently credits me with getting the ball rolling for that role, and I'm proud of that accomplishment. Years later, I learned firsthand what a difference it makes. My daughter had a stroke, and our Patient Navigator was absolutely essential as we figured out how to move forward during her post-stroke recovery. I never thought my work would come full circle to benefit my family, but that experience drove home the importance of both the hospital and the role.

"Since the relationship is personal, I respond quickly when one of my favorite organizations asks me to support their mission. They get the money right away. Sometimes I'll also write what I call 'just because' checks, especially for something to benefit the people who are doing the work. I do it just because I can, and because they make me feel good."

Where's the Starting Point?

It's easy to read a book and get excited for a moment in time. However, if this book is actually going to drive change, then action must follow the enthusiasm.

I know this approach seems counterintuitive to many people. I recently was talking to a nonprofit executive who had just one and a half staff. She asked me how she could find the time to take this approach with her limited resources.

So I broke it down for her. I asked how many significant donors the organization currently had in its fold. She responded that about 20-25 knew the organization and had capacity. That made it relatively easy to suggest a starting point.

First, I suggested she meet with one donor each week over the next several months. She could talk about how the organization is meeting its mission today, and its vision for the future. Once this initial opener question set the stage, she could begin asking open-ended questions about the donor's greatest interests in the work.

I also suggested that after each meeting, she jot down two or three actionable steps that would further engage that donor. It might be something as simple as attending a program, taking a tour, or attending a small dinner party with like-minded donors. I reminded her that each cultivation pathway would be different.

I then asked how many of her donors had capacity but didn't know the organization well. Again, she responded with about the same number. I suggested that during the next few months, while she was interviewing the more cultivated donors, that she look for a few pollinators that might know the less cultivated donors. Two or three pollinators would be enough to make the difference in this case. Those pollinators could help develop the cultivation pathways for the less connected donors by reviewing the list and supplying essential information about the donor's interests.

One of my early mentors once said, "Starve your problems and feed your opportunities." I'm so grateful I heeded that advice as a young fundraising professional, because it has held me in good stead for more than thirty years. It's as true for anyone involved in a nonprofit organization as it was for me. As organizations become more confident in the success of this process, they realize it's time to prioritize those activities that feed opportunities for greater fundraising success. It's also time to let go of the activities that have great cost but produce little or no return on investment.

From the Toolshed

Let's see if it's time to move forward. Answer the following questions (honestly!) on a scale of 1-5, with 1 being "Not true at all" and 5 being "Completely true."

- Gifts to the organization have plateaued and we don't know exactly how to increase them.
- It feels like our organization is in a rut. We don't know how to engage our donors.
- Our organization hasn't seen the kind of gift increases that our donor community is capable of making.
- It feels like our organization is going through the motions and mechanics of transactional fundraising.
- Our organization feels pressure to make our annual operating budget and we don't know how to make up the difference between what we have and what we need.

Now total up the score. You could have a minimum score of 5, and a maximum score of 25. The higher the score, the more something needs to change …and soon!

Let's do the same exercise with a different set of questions.

- Our organization does amazing work.
- There's untapped opportunity to raise money for our organization.

- Our organization should have better, more productive relationships with its board and its committee members.

If your organization has a high score here (and I bet it does) then there's hope for far greater fundraising success. Simply return to Chapter One and start implementing the strategies I've outlined in this book.

While the suggestions I've made might seem challenging to implement, remember to break it down like I did for that nonprofit executive and take the steps slowly. Most organizations take six months or a year to transition from transactional fundraising to relationship-based fundraising. Because the work is new, it can feel clumsy in the beginning. But the return on investment is great. Remember the quote from Executive Director Melanie earlier in this book. "Once the system was set up and we took it for a spin, we saw remarkable, continuous results."

If more resources or more help are needed, I would also suggest reading all the way to Chapter 10. There are some great fertilizers listed in that chapter that can help with your organization's work.

NINE: REFLECTIONS OF A GARDENER

"A garden is a grand teacher. It teaches patience and careful watchfulness; it teaches industry and thrift; above all it teaches entire trust."

— Gertrude Jekyll, 19th Century Horticulturist

I wouldn't call myself an expert gardener in any sense of the word. However, I do enjoy growing fresh herbs. Through that hobby, I have learned how important it is to care for plants individually.

I made some rookie mistakes the first year. I put mint in the same pot as the other herbs. If you've ever grown mint, you know how this story goes. Of course, the mint completely took over and choked out everything else. I learned that if I give all herbs the same amount of water and sun, oregano and dill die quickly. Some herbs need to be harvested regularly. Others need to be pruned in order to thrive. Now, a few years into my hobby, I've become much more adept. I give each herb the individualized plan of care it needs to thrive. I'm happier, my herbs are growing nicely, and my cooking has benefitted, too!

We've been exploring the idea of customized cultivation pathways throughout this book. Donors are not a group. Each one is an individual. They all have personal stories and reasons why they might connect to your organization. When an organization focuses in on major donors with a personalized plan of cultivation, their gifts will grow. Just as I did with my herbs, your organization will also learn from its mistakes.

Does this mean your organization should never send out another newsletter? Absolutely not! It's important to share success stories with all donors, and a newsletter is a great way to communicate efficiently with a large audience. Just remember that tactics such as newsletters and annual appeals are probably not going to increase inclination among top donor prospects. A letter only works for the person for whom a letter works.

What about hosting the event du jour? In the 80s, bowl-a-thons were the hot thing. Then auctions, followed by golf outings, showed up on every nonprofit fundraising calendar. Each decade seems to have a trendy fundraising event. Should your organization follow suit? It depends. A donor acquisition golf event, for example, makes all the sense in the world when fundraising for an historic golf course. But a golf outing that is not mission-connected is probably not the best strategy. It's important to choose a donor acquisition event that connects inclined donors to the mission and work of the organization.

I've spent more than thirty years in fundraising. And before that, I spent fourteen years in sales. My orientation was then, as it is now, to build individual relationships. I have seen the most success with the clients who focus on each significant donor as an individual. When they figure out why that donor cares about the mission, and what they can do to deepen the connection, the gifts come more naturally and more often.

~ An Illustration ~

As I just mentioned, fundraising was actually a second career for me. My first career was in sales. I spent fourteen years learning to build client relationships in order to drive revenue. Each one of those relationships was unique. Although I didn't think of it in those terms back then, I was a gardener, cultivating my little patch of client flowers.

Then I started my fundraising career at the local branch of a national nonprofit. Who knew that philanthropy (at the time) was different than sales? I found a lot less individual cultivation and a lot more aggregate techniques.

The fundraising methodology at my first nonprofit job followed a strict formula. They put envelopes in neighborhood mailboxes, and then a volunteer picked them up. They also sent an annual appeal letter, hosted a run, and held one major fundraising event each year.

Don't get me wrong…they did fairly well with this approach. They raised a lot of money, mostly in $5-$10 increments, occasionally a bit more (remember this was in the mid-90s). But when I started looking at the results of the year-end appeal letter, I found some $500 checks. Those were huge, especially back then.

I immediately clicked back into sales mode. My thought was, "These people have true interest in our cause. Maybe if we got to know them a bit better, we could improve our results even more! After all, there aren't that many of them." I was firmly, albeit politely, told that that was not how we did things at this organization.

That's the way it was thirty years ago…but not today! Today, we know that fundraising is more dynamic. Transactional fundraising is a thing of the past, not the trend for the future.

The Lesson: I learned very early in my nonprofit career that donors should be treated as individuals. We need to understand what the mission means to them, and how their experiences connect to us. We can't just rely on events and a year-end appeal to meet the annual and long-term needs of the organization.

~

The Roots of This Methodology

The content in this book reflects my thirty-plus years of philanthropy experience. As with many "how to" books, it didn't start out as a coherent, comprehensive plan. I really started codifying my thoughts and processes after the recession of 2008. I didn't set out to write a book at that time. I was just trying to help clients understand the trends I was seeing. The Greatest Generation was no longer at the forefront of the donor prospect pool. In their stead, the Baby Boomers were making their giving decisions based on fundraising best practices and program impact. So from 2008-2010, I focused on systematizing an approach to individual donor cultivation. That sounds counterintuitive, but that's what it is.

Since that time, this system has flourished. We put it to the test in 2020 with the pandemic. I'm happy to report that it's thriving! The clients who have our system in place are doing well. They found that donors and donor prospects were more available for virtual meetings during the pandemic than they ever were for face-to-face meetings. As a result, they moved even faster to achieve fundraising goals. Our clients who run a relationship-based model of philanthropy are also more flexible and resilient. They don't rely on the transactional, one-size-fits-all approach. They quickly pivoted to virtual activities that kept donors connected to the mission. Their donors are sticking with them, and they are continuing to garner support. I won't ever say the pandemic was good, but I can say it was good for individual fundraising!

Organizations that didn't have personalized relationships basically sat out through the pandemic. Sadly, I can guess what will happen to many of them if the "traditional event" drought continues. Many of them will cease to exist, or cut their services back to the barest of bones, just as in 2008. Who knows if they will ever recover?

It's Never Too Late

I'm now decades into this career, and I've worked with literally hundreds of nonprofit organizations. But I must confess that it still surprises me when I encounter a sophisticated, seemingly put-together organization that uses the old transactional approach. I guess I shouldn't be so stunned. It's easy to become complacent if fundraising goals can be met without digging too deep.

I remember one event for which I purchased a ticket myself — I didn't attend as someone's guest or because they were a client. I bought a ticket because I cared that much about the cause. I landed on their mailing list, but they never dug deep enough to find out what drew me to their mission or to cultivate my interest. That was actually disappointing. I would like to have been cultivated!

I've also attended events as a guest of another donor. I've made gifts. In some cases, I've gone back repeatedly. Many of those organizations have never contacted me. That's very disappointing, because I know I'm not the only donor who was ignored after showing interest at an event.

All that being said, don't give up, even if your organization has made some of these mistakes! It's never too late to take a different approach. It's not rocket science, but it does take time and energy. However, do it for the right reasons. In other words, don't do this just to raise more money. Donors will see right through that façade. Instead, take this approach because it creates a rich donor experience with your organization.

Here's the reward. The process of creating individual cultivation pathways and rich donor experiences will lead to larger gifts. Your organization will come to realize, as I have for many years, that we find our greatest fulfillment as philanthropy professionals and fundraising volunteers when donor hearts connect to organizational missions. *That's* why we do this work!

From the Toolshed

I hope that this book inspires you to pull on some gloves, grab a shovel, and get to work on a donor garden for your organization!

Here are some great resources I can suggest for more information:
- *The Tipping Point: How Little Things Can Make a Big Difference* by Malcolm Gladwell. This book introduces the idea of mavens, salespeople, and pollinators in the

for-profit world. I borrowed and repurposed those titles in Chapter Five, but you will gain more context around this idea from reading the whole book.

- *Asking: A 59-Minute Guide to Everything Board Members, Volunteers, and Staff Must Know to Secure the Gift* by Jerold Panas. Yes, I know this one has been out for a while. But it is an extremely worthwhile book…a classic that I refer to time and again.
- *Conducting a Successful Capital Campaign: The New, Revised, and Expanded Edition of the Leading Guide to Planning and Implementing a Capital Campaign* by Kent Dove. Again, this is another of those "oldie but goodie" books. Someone gave me a copy when I was involved in my first campaign, and I still think it's the definitive work on the subject.
- Fundkit (www.getfundkit.com). Kennari Consulting, the firm I started, provides personalized consulting for nonprofit organizations. This toolkit has arisen from our work. It's designed to help nonprofit professionals and board members take a deep, step-by-step dive into some of the most fundamental fundraising processes that are essential to success. Each course features a series of video lessons, downloadable resources, and next steps. It's a cost-effective way for self-starters to benefit from expert coaching.